Volume 81 of the Yale Series of Younger Poets

Terms to Be Met

GEORGE
BRADLEY

Foreword by
James Merrill

Yale University Press
New Haven and London

Publication of this volume was made possible
by a gift from The Guinzberg Fund.

Designed by Sally Harris
and set in Meridien type by
The Composing Room of Michigan, Inc.
Printed in the United States of America by
Halliday Lithograph, West Hanover, Massachusetts.

Library of Congress Cataloging-in-Publication Data

Bradley, George, 1953–
  Terms to be met.

  (Volume 81 of the Yale series of younger poets)
  I. Title.   II. Series: Yale series of younger
poets ; v. 81.
PS3552.R227T47   1986   811'.54   85–22584
ISBN 0–300–03598–5 (alk. paper)
ISBN 0–300–03599–3 (pbk. : alk. paper)

The paper in this book meets the guidelines for
permanence and durability of the Committee on
Production Guidelines for Book Longevity
of the Council on Library Resources.

10   9   8   7   6   5   4   3   2   1

Contents

1301921

Foreword

In the air, at thirty thousand feet or so, we keep to ourselves: make notes, watch a film, prefer the company of clouds. "Inwardness hangs aloft," as John Hollander put it. To the good old days of railroad travel belong the compulsive talkers with their family stories and snapshots. Here's Velma before she and Fred broke up; here we are with our youngest at the Petrified Forest. Now that trains are being phased out, what's become of those self-delighting chatterers? Are they being phased out, too? Not on your life. They are writing poetry.

George Bradley takes a firm stand against all this. As if we opened a book in order to meet the people next door! Love poems? Not really; the *you* he presents is, more often than not, a modest surrogate *I* who forestalls voyeurism by inviting the reader into his thought. Personal history, what it means to numberless poets harvesting it even as I draft this sentence, is simply put on hold. "Leaving Kansas City," whether or not its author began there, he strikes out, with his back turned also upon the prevailing poetic manners of the heartland, for Bruges and Byzantium, for lofty places and long views, Colorado, the Himalayas, "M31 in Andromeda." Yet it will not do to complain that his poems lack human interest. It is with the human interest precisely of inwardness that they quiver—the ongoing adventure, the world as meditation.

Emblems punctuate the book: a globe and an hourglass, shapes which accord well with Bradley's travels in space and time. The opening poem may not be *shaped* like a bridge, but its form—through end-words which attain the middle line's "summit" only to repeat themselves in reverse or descending order—enacts the little triumph of engineering, as one might call any span's metaphorical dimension:

> The structure of our adventure, the road
> We went by, protected us from the view
> Beneath us,

until, on the river's far side, setting us

> down out of the sky
> According to the prescriptions of our beginning
> Into a difficult place, though we weren't particular.

"Prescriptions" as of a destiny written, say genetically, *before* it is lived; "protected" as one must be if the quest is to succeed; "the view / Beneath us" in both senses of the phrase. Finally, "though we weren't particular" conveys at once self-effacement, indifference—the road is everything, where it leads hardly matters—and some trace element of necessity: even though we've traveled light, left behind the particular in favor of the essential, observed, in short, the poetics of *this* adventure, the end remains "a difficult place," the last act is always bloody. Touch by touch, Bradley's language, at first glance plain as the Kansas his next poem will be driving us through, begins to shimmer like a mirage. Midway through his book, or nearly, and at the heart of his "globe," where Dante placed Satan, Bradley plants a colon: the tiny doubled point standing for the wobble inherent in our most lucid views, or the dazzle that besets our least abandoned diction.

"Leaving Kansas City" goes beyond the dry humor of

> On the only radio station, a voice explains,
> In an accent you wouldn't have thought possible,
> The most practical way of doing something
> It would never have occurred to you to do,

past these notes artlessly wistful as a cowboy's guitar:

> You move on because somewhere up ahead,
> If you remember right, if you're going the right way,
> If everything they told you was true . . .
> There is a place called Colorado

and concludes with a passage that links—another bridge—the westward impulse of our forebears to the no less instinctive one which (like the conquistadors' El Dorado, Cavafy's Ithaka, and Proust's Venice) locates in our own imaginations the places we yearn for.

Bradley is perhaps too much at home in a secondary world, but who makes the rules? In attempting to fathom the primary one, we need all the help we can get. Old painters and architects stand guard over this book, as do Marianne Moore and Wallace Stevens. Cavafy comes through as an example more fruitful yet, with his singularly unmetaphorical language and deft explorations of creative strategy. Now can be glimpsed the human figures we might have missed elsewhere: Fayoum casket portraits, Socrates, Galileo, Brunelleschi, even "the old poet" himself "at our café" in an Alexandria established by his latest disciple as properly fictive from the start. Glimpses only, trick perspectives—what trouble with the here and now makes a poet cling to such devices?

For one thing, they reinforce the mind forever haunted by collapse and erosion, like the dome of Hagia Sophia or the rock formations in Monument Valley. Descent from the "summit" of any mental span is inescapable. So is art's patchwork aspect, which, says Bradley with lovely forbearance (note the play on "content"),

> arises out of a chance accumulation,
> Out of a mind that perhaps achieved optimum content
> Months or even years ago, say one morning in winter
> When the sky was so blue and steam rose off the ocean
> Into the other element of air.

Then too, a thoughtful poet will want to check the rush of sensation. "Feelings and images," wrote Camus, "multiply a philosophy by ten." All the more reason to use them sparingly. At times the very realities that most interest Bradley require "the mirror images of scientific equipment." The naked eye, or indeed its naked homophone, can make nothing of "M31 in Andromeda." But give a man a telescope, this poem seems to say, and he will tell you the truth about his inmost psyche:

> Stellar Body M31 was long remarked for an odd imbalance,
> Revolving in mysterious concert with its own dark motives.
> The hidden motivation turns out to be ourselves, our Milky Way,
> . . . .
> The great gathering of light spins majestically in space,
> Centrifugal force and the force of gravity conspiring
> To yield configuration, an elegant ellipse, though why
> To turn in emptiness, in absence of light or any warmth,
> Should form anything is not easy to imagine, any more than why
> Our own thoughts and dreams should take shape out of darkness.

The message, familiar since Greek tragedy, is plain: man is himself both marvel and monster. As the poem concludes, the relevant myth surfaces:

> it seems Andromeda
> Was a woman so beautiful she was set out on a rock, bound
> Beside the sea and with a sea of stars over her head,
> There to satisfy something terrible, something that no one,
> Not her father, who was king, nor her father's priests,
> Nor we who read the tale, had any real hope of averting
> Or could think to comprehend.

This must be the only version of the Andromeda story in which her savior Perseus fails to materialize—except that he has already done so, as the artist-scientist turning his mirror shield upon the mystery. By these last lines the "extraordinarily beautiful" galaxy has merged with the doomed princess. So has that "something terrible" with "ourselves, our Milky Way." ("Our Milky Way"—doesn't the phrase give out some glimmering of our performance as mammals?) The connections are drawn gravely yet companionably. It is all worth hearing, and Bradley doesn't patronize us with gimmicks or grimaces in the telling.

We have grown used, in all the arts, to a spasmodic, Dionysian approach to experience, with points for a hot vocabulary, "involvement" and "witness"—the red shoes of the actual, twitching by themselves, to no music worth the name. In such a context Apollonian measures are welcome, especially at the hands of a poet able first of all to hear the interval between cosmos and psyche, then skillful enough to strike pianissimo that vital octave:

> If you listen closely some morning, when the sun swells
> Over the horizon and the world is still and still asleep,
> You might hear it, a faint noise so far inside your mind
> That it must come from somewhere, from light rushing to darkness,
> Energy burning towards entropy, towards a peaceful solution,
> Burning brilliantly, spontaneously, in the middle of nowhere,
> And you, too, must make a sound that is somewhat like it,
> Though that, of course, you have no way of hearing at all.

What impresses is the wide, sure orbit by which such conclusions are reached. That Bradley's so often appear foregone means in part his sensible reluctance to break new ground indiscriminately, in part that he has attained that rightness of wording which is a poet's best chance of being remembered.

James Merrill

Acknowledgments

Some of the poems in this book first appeared in the following publications:

The American Poetry Review: "Lights of Assisi"
American Review: "Leaving Kansas City"
Antaeus: "E Pur Si Muove"
Grand Street: "Its Bladder-Like Sail"
The New Yorker: "Christ Pantocrator in San Giorgio dei Greci"
The Paris Review: "The Sound of the Sun," "In Suspense,"
    "Caskets in the Fayoum"
Partisan Review: "Aubade," "Monument Valley"
Poetry: "Committed to Memory," "An Arrangement of Sunlight
    at Hagia Sophia"
Seneca Review: "M31 in Andromeda," "Terms to Be Met"
Shenandoah: "A Palaeologan Apology," "Filippo Brunelleschi,
    Florence, 1425," "In the Himalayas," "Light Falls on the
    Man," "In the Flemish Gallery," "The Life of Stars"
The Yale Review: "Three People Reading Stevens in a Room"

I

In Suspense

at the Verrazano Narrows Bridge

The composition of many particulars
Held the broad promise of our beginning
And so we set out calmly into the sky,
Out over sheer space and distant waters
Where other travellers had found harbor;
It was the gothic grandeur, the bright towers,
By which we knew the magnitude of our attempt,
Rushing forward into the expanding light.
The structure of our adventure, the road
We went by, protected us from the view
Beneath us, and it was the monumental
Objects, distant caricatures of themselves,
Which tried to occupy our attention.
Having come so far, we reached the summit:
A surprise, we hadn't been paying attention
To much besides a perception of ourselves
As puny and audacious, caught in a monumental
Undertaking; but now the panoramic view
Of our accomplishment, the end of the road,
Presented itself in the soft, reflected light.
We felt, of course, elevated in our attempt,
Inspired by the reach of the last aspiring tower,
Felt fulfilled in the wish each of us harbors
To journey and return safely off the waters;
And so we were set down out of the sky
According to the prescriptions of our beginning
Into a difficult place, though we weren't particular.

Leaving Kansas City

Kansas City depends a lot on the way
You look at it. If you approach from the West,
It takes on a certain weary beauty:
Misguided, uninspired, familiar.
But driving through from the East,
It's just another group of grubby people
After you thought you'd passed all that.

Lying partly on ground that considered
Being a bluff, and partly on the plain,
It's a city where different states are possible
For people who don't often get that kind of choice.
In the middle, running nowhere from nowhere,
Is the Missouri, a river that moves off
Like a lake that got a little restless.
There are a few office buildings, from the late
Thirties, which is when the government stopped
Giving them away, and when folks here stopped
Worrying about keeping up with the times.
The city pumps out smog, absentmindedly,
Because that is what big cities do.

You didn't know you loved it till you left it;
From now on there isn't much of anything:
Several towns like Abilene, which mean a lot
In the movies, and one or two ghost towns,
If you want to be where other people
Decided not to be. Steadily, inexorably,
The desolation opens out in front of you . . .
There is some satisfaction in realizing
That it's just as bad as you heard it was.
The sun burns everything jackrabbit brown,
And nothing grows high enough to be noticed.
Infrequently, and in questionable taste,

There are garish green spots of irrigation
Where someone just gave it up and stayed.
Before long you have travelled to the point
Where it would be pointless to turn back.

The next point of reference is twenty miles off,
An ill-defined part of the horizon,
A slight rise like the one twenty miles back.
You find so much ground to pass over
That covering it quickly isn't much help.
On the only radio station, a voice explains,
In an accent you wouldn't have thought possible,
The most practical way of doing something
It would never have occurred to you to do.
The voice is distant and doesn't seem aimed at you.

By now you've lost track of precisely
What you had in mind. You move on because
For some reason you have come here to do that,
Although what you are doing is completely
Unremarkable. You wouldn't know to look around,
But they take this route every day; incredibly,
People far worse equipped than yourself
Did the same thing a long time ago.
You move on because somewhere up ahead,
If you remember right, if you're going the right way,
If everything they told you was true . . .
There is a place called Colorado where you will,
Of course, be very glad to arrive, where the others
Wanted to go; and you will sit smug in the shade
High up on a mountain, feeling the wind
Send shivers over your body, looking back
At the great sickening swoop of the plain
And think it part of a grand design:
Satisfying, necessary, even beautiful.

Monument Valley

Maybe the mind works like centuries of erosion,
The runoffs and channels mostly bone-dry and then flooded
With a wall of water out of the desert, itself absorbed
Almost instantly into the cracked ground and leaving
Only a thin layer of fine sludge like a train of thought.
Over time the larger formations appear, personality
And prejudice, a manner of speaking, assuming all sorts
Of fantastic shapes, climbing into the atmosphere
And achieving a shimmering air of grandeur and intent.
Of course, much is washed away that these may remain,
And the landscape of youth is ravaged beneath us.
Whatever is extraneous, or delicate, or less than tenacious,
Has less chance than a pack rat in the progress of ages,
Less chance than our own acts and inmost reflections
Stand in a lifetime of vanishing memories.
And we are left with monuments, resembling so much,
To soften the harsh light into shadows and their hues,
To make something like beauty out of such earth.

Aubade

Once in a great while, you might open your eyes
Into bright sunlight and think you are somewhere else.
Say Sardegna in '76, early one morning in Olbia—
The sun is red and huge, rising over the bay,
And the day is already warm; the town is weathered,
Worn to the colors of a pastel sketch, like the eyes
Of a man who has been drunk most of his life—
Bleached by the sun, or washed out by memory? There
Is no way of knowing, and of course you can never go back.
To speak the same words, to stand the same ground
Will not suffice, and the thought itself accomplishes
Nothing. All of it, Olbia, that sun, yourself one morning,
Is whirling away like the speed of light, and you
Are borne into a life irretrievably infused with a reality
Beyond recall, so that there is no telling how you arrived
In the sunshine, confused, waking as from dreams.

Lights of Assisi

You wake one afternoon in an accustomed city—
There is a dog barking; children are somewhere—
Suspicious that whatever you came to see
Doesn't care either now. Landscapes, wherever,
Have gone pretty vague: the heat leaves a haze
Not immediately apparent, accumulating in the distance.
You await the demystification of darkness.

Pinpoints of light, preoccupied, follow paths
Of precise variation—small cars whining out of sight—
There is, then, some connection with your scene.
Now that the sun has gone and matters are settled,
Fainter configurations beckon out of the blackness:
Lights shine, flicker like a brushfire, like stars.
It is meant to be a wonderful city, dedicated

To a man who managed to love what was around him.
You think your desires, too, are fashioned
As they are perceived, merely habitations
Seen at the limits of vision; like these lights
Illuminating a site no doubt as dark as your own,
Where children contemplate the fruit trees
And old men talk in whispers with the birds.

Via del Bovaro

The bell tower near the courtyard
   Where we spent that year,
Perched at the edge of Perugia,
   Housed tireless engines
Of consumption, insatiable swifts.

The birds wheeled through every instant
   Of the daylight hours,
Darting and diving after what
   We could not see—gnats,
Midges, mosquitoes—their piercing cries

Filling the blank sky of summer
   As their motion filled
The foreground of a scene that ran
   Before us off to
Paradise, or at least Assisi.

We paid them little mind, our thoughts
   Given over to
Meals, *moda*, trysts and *tristezza*,
   Words learned new each night,
The terms we found for first attachments—

Gina, Astrid, Antonio,
   Garth, Ann and others—
Sharing all, even cigarettes,
   We tried to carry
On in the International Style;

Mostly, of course, sheer chance threw us
   Together, as chance
Has since tossed us apart, each one
   Reabsorbed in his
Own particulars and point of view.

The view we shared that year was grand,
   Was breathtaking, but
When I recall the time and place
   (How the mind circles
Beautifully back), what I see there,

Mostly, are the swifts, hungering
   Over Umbria,
The lines they draw in air like lines
   In shadowed mirrors
Where we stare at what we have become.

San Miniato al Monte

Walking into sunlight, shedding centuries
   That gather in the church behind you,
It all seems plain as day, the streets and small squares
Spread before your eyes like the palm of your hand,
   Like the guidebook's illustrated view.
You determine points of public interest,
The Duomo, the rusticated palaces,
   And locate some private landmarks, too:
There is that o.k. trattoria, and there
The pensione where mosquitoes worried
   You all night, and where a woman—who?
Yes, that's right—left you for reasons still unclear,
Though clearly not unusual, leaving with
   One or two remarks that might be true.
Remember how the little towns on the hilltops
Around the city looked on as they look now,
   How memories came out of the blue
And hovered over the tile roofs like a haze,
The scene shimmering as the sky does with heat?
   You felt the tide of affairs flow through
You like a river that wells at intervals
To leap broad embankments, only to recede
   Days later, leaving a residue
Of refuse, mud, and incidental damage;
And you felt, too, your mind searching the rubble
   For whatever there was to rescue.
What could be found was more than could be recalled,
Or so it seems now . . . perhaps just this city,
   A thing of sentimental value
With its beauty, its ancient fabrications.
Wonderful how meaning attaches itself
   To what there is, wonderful how two
People in conversation can so affect
Their surroundings, even over years, even
   At this remove, wonderful, and you
Start downward, the city rising at your side.

Where the Blue Begins

In the southern Adriatic, where the blue begins,
We came to rest awhile and play
On sun-drenched islands known as Tremiti,
Where the breeze blows fresh
And pine trees shiver and the salt sea
Washes the likes of you and me,
In the southern Adriatic, in the wind-blown spray.
In the bluest water, just where it begins,
We came to play awhile, came to rest
On rocky shores of barren coves,
As the swells arrived and water splashed
And reflected sunlight jumped and shimmered
Among the cliffs and overhangs and grottoes,
In the Adriatic, where that sort of thing begins.
In the clear blue water that the swells bring by
Out of the sunny Adriatic Sea,
We came to rest and play and bathe ourselves,
As the pine trees swayed on the bluffs above
And wind dispersed the salt sea spray,
In the sunny Adriatic, where a way of life begins.
We came seeking an immersion, to find ourselves
In waters clear enough to fathom
A bottom profoundly blue, to see it seemed
All the way to Greece or any other site
That water washed as well or sun could so ignite,
Came to see ourselves in a world of dreams,
That words might furnish what place implies,
That place might finish what a word begins.
We came seeking clearest water, sunniest sky,
Came, you and I, to see what would be seen
Immersed in waters consummately blue,
In sunlit swells that carried their dark secret,
Tiny hosts known as *meduse*, whose fragile arms

Glanced and stung and burned all day
And raised the blush that blossomed on our skins,
Aggravated by the sun and spray,
By our own attempts to hold each other,
As we swam out of ourselves and were swept away,
In the southern Adriatic, where the blue begins.

A Nice Place to Visit

I have never been to Alexandria, where
The desert meets the Mareotic Lake and birds
Hover the day long above the old marketplace.
I have never travelled where the sand disappears
Amidst the wet confusion that the Nile becomes,
Never where hot winds bring clouds up off the ocean
And send them scudding over the antique setting.
I have not been there, although I have encompassed
Alexandria, circling that well-known city,
So that if you fixed a foot there at Egypt's edge
And set a radius of, say, five hundred miles,
I have been almost anyplace you put the point;
Almost any place, but not Alexandria,
Where night falls quickly over the empty desert,
And distant lights in the shipping lanes shine brightly
Across the water like a city out at sea.

These cities must remain as I imagine them,
The one at sea, the real one beside the harbor,
But Alexandria is still what I call home,
And already I start to feel sad and homesick
Because the city isn't what it used to be.
Oh yes, I know the romance has gone out of it,
That those expatriates have all gone somewhere else,
And that Greek isn't spoken there at all these days;
But my dishevelled city is where the heart lies,
And that is home—not Athens, with its discothèques,
Nor Rome, with its motor scooters and high crime rate—
But Alexandria, lackluster by the sea.

Today is a good day for visiting, because
Saint Mark will be holding forth before the palace,
And one or two Ptolemys will attend his words.
The great library will surely catch fire today,
Now that the British have begun shelling the town,
But there will be a diplomatic bash tonight
Just the same, and business will be back to normal—
Slaves, guns, ivory—tomorrow in the bazaar.
This evening, we can meet once more at our café,
Where the liquor is cheap and comes in clean glasses,
And where we can watch the old poet fall in love
With the waiter all over again; afterwards,
We'll walk down near the harbor, the air so balmy,
The breeze and just a little dust ruffling our hair,
And you'll be starry-eyed, so impressed, and I'll be
So glad to show you Alexandria, my home.

What the Magi Knew

"Light attracts light, fleeing from the dark,
    that is why you come to me,"
      said the Parsee priest
as a bright sun set over Bombay,
    distinguishing benighted
      millions in its rays.
India Gate caught the evening light,
    and the sky caught fire as we
      discussed what may be
the oldest faith held anywhere on earth,
    Zoroastrianism,
      what the magi knew.
The two of us took tea together:
    an old man pale as parchment,
      wearing white linen
and dressed in the cloth of his belief;
    and his foreign visitor,
      dressed in ignorance
and the clothes of another climate,
    bearing a consular note
      of introduction.
"The closest thing we find in nature
    to divinity is light,
      and its form is fire,"
continued my aged host, a man
    learned in prophetic texts
      and commentaries,
"yet mere flames are not what we revere;
    they are an image of God,
      a divine idea."
Beyond the roof where we were sitting,
    past Victoria Station
      and across Back Bay,

the lights in the British Residence
        on top of Malabar Hill
            came on one by one
and shone on a windowless stone shape
        that stood in stark silhouette
            on the ridge below.
The curiosity that brought me
        made me ask. "Tell me," I said,
            "about the tower."
"The light must not be mixed with darkness,"
        replied my tutor, shifting
            in his seat, shifting
his regard to gaze out at the sea,
        out towards the ships that make
            the city what it is.
"For this reason, we do not mix with
        Hindu; for this reason we
            do not burn our dead.
And it is not right to put sickness
        in the soil, so we do not
            put our dead in earth.
Instead, when the light has left the eyes,
        and the soul has flown out of
            the body, we take
our dead to the tower of silence."
        The old Parsee sipped his tea,
            returning his eyes
to me. "But always there are fewer,"
        he said. "We are less each day,
            and those most in need
of an introduction to our faith
        are our own people, our young.
            Each day we are less,
and we do not practice as before.
        Our ceremonies require
            an eternal flame,

but these days the scented woods are rare,
    and many cannot afford
        sandalwood and teak;
so it is that we must worship God
    with whatever can be found,
        refuse from Bombay."
Palladian dilapidations
    seemed to comprehend his words,
        architectural
reminders of a state in decay,
    the state of empire dissolved
        in monsoons and gin.
Beyond Back Bay, the stone shape grew dim,
    dissolving with the daylight.
        The shape lacked a roof,
strange in a city with so much rain.
    "Tell me," I said, "what happens
        inside the tower."
Jamshid Cawaji Katrak, a man
    who knew what the magi might
        have known, weighed his words.
"Purely a sanitary measure,"
    he said after a pause. "Why
        must you know these things?
When I am dead, those who love me best
    will bear me to the tower
        and place my body
on a slab of marble to await
    the birds of death, offering
        my corpse to the sky.
When the elements and scavengers
    have done their work, when ravens
        have picked my bones clean,
what remains, and it will be little,
    becomes part of the tower,
        put into its walls.

Afterwards, the ones I love will burn
    incense in the temple fire,
        giving my soul life."
Around the rooftop where we conversed,
    the night advanced. The sun lay
        hull-down in the sea,
and twilight introduced its shadows
    into each face and window.
        "Will you have more tea?"
asked Jamshid Cawaji. "Then go, please.
    It grows late, and nowadays
        I tire easily.
Tonight, I compose an article
    concerning the marriage rites
        of ancient Persia.
Arabic scholars have accused us
    of practicing bigamy,
        as they do themselves,
but I shall demonstrate otherwise;
    their own lies will refute them.
        Dark gathers darkness,
which is why we fled Arabia.
    Go now. What more would you know?
        Take my thoughts with you:
our days are as a fire before God,
    and though the image dwindles,
        the idea remains."
Go, he said, and I did, descending
    through the black streets of Bombay,
        pursuing my way
into other cities, carrying
    those bright words and walking with
        darkness all my days.

In the Himalayas

Someone has built a stairway to the sky, and we climb
Slowly, followed thousands of feet by the swift sound
Of the river running through the gorge below us.
It is lovely labor to be accepted into the clouds,
And as mere walking is hard work, someone has paved
A pathway and flagged a set of steps into the hillside.
Below us lies a landscape of such radical proportions
That it has consumed a day's difficult journey
To discover what distances the eye can see.
The surrounding mist eddies and sometimes separates
To reveal a section of snowbound rockface, seen
At an acute angle, immediately and amazingly above us.
From our vantage point, the mountains spring
Another twenty thousand feet, as suddenly as doorposts.

In my country, countryside so high would be barren,
But in these latitudes the vegetation remains lush:
A dense jungle complete with a canopy of creepers,
With ferns and hanging moss and troops of monkeys
Making more noise than I had imagined monkeys made.
The air is heavy with a familiar presence, too pervasive
To be easily remembered, but recognized at last
For rhododendron trees: a forest full of them!
The echo of an axe tells us what work is done
Below the monasteries and above the terraced fields.
No one inherits his buffalo and half-acre here;
Instead the only birthright is the body itself,
The tireless limbs and enormous lung capacity.

In a rhythm of exertion and strained exhilaration
We pursue our uneven struggle, for in this remote world
Whatever descends is most inclined to ascend again.
Out of our depth, like fish out of water, we gasp

And suffer symptoms: headaches, nausea, swollen joints.
As sleep comes to the man at ease in his environs,
We lie uncomfortably awake in the hours before dawn.
In our exhaustion, and in these unforeseen circumstances,
We dream by day, are coolly rational only in the dark.

A week's walk brings us to a tiny retreat
Of small ceremony, containing old inscriptions
Written in a dying language. A glance is sufficient;
We leave the monks in their crude red robes,
Leave the lunar landscape of the Tibetan plateau,
And return the many miles home by another way.

It is the dreamed experience of a lifetime, though
These observations will leave us few in the future;
The mountains are a magnificence too much for memory,
And we are changed irreparably in inexplicable moments
(Dhaulagiri filling the sky from forty miles away,
The snow sailing from its peak up in the jet stream).
And this is the bourn from which so little is returned,
The instant of our understanding, its massive impact
Faster than shutter speed, like the pierce of emotion,
An evanescence understood almost as love, bursting
As one thought leads to the next.

II

Life as We Know It

Here aboard this

crude shape sailing through space,

with impressions impinging from all angles, like

starlight, always and all at once, and the lightyears from

where we stand to the limits of our understanding, the borders

of invisibility that put an end to our surmises, in all directions

roughly equidistant, although it doesn't appear so unconsidered—the

shape of our perceptions is spherical, and a good thing, too. Perhaps

it could be formulated empirically: Radius, or Reach, is Intelligence by

Persistence by Situation, but in any case the form's just right, tough

enough to take almost anything, retentive and resistant and slipping

through space on a path to a cold end as inanimate mass, long into

the future and many circles from now, reflecting into darkness

and trailing wisps of atmosphere like the ambiance of lost

days that we require, that we are losing always,

our medium, our support, of us and

our   definition.

Caskets in the Fayoum

Everybody has a point of view,
    a public expression when
        all is said and done,
and each man is his own achievement,
    even in, if only in,
        the bland face of death.
Here, at this remote oasis where
    a desert stretches away
        to eternity,
tourists don't often tour, their flashbulbs
    unable to shed much light
        on caves and caskets
where the dead lay down with their beliefs
    to be made a spectacle,
        made the spectators.
Wide-eyed and incredulous, each one
    looks oddly startled by death,
        surprised in the act,
and each portrait, fixed in encaustic,
    preserves a final instant
        when the hot wax cooled.
Yannis (these faces have lost their names,
    but I return them, harmless
        words of convenience)
peers placidly out of his dim past
    into our dark forever;
        notice the slight smile:
he was happy perhaps and died young.
    Thea, though, had had enough;
        bejewelled and be-chinned,
she knew how other people saw her
    and couldn't care; she finds us
        as unattractive

in our day as our kind were in hers.
We give others our regards:
Manos, with one eye,
though it's wide and wondrous all the same;
Maria, who's just a child
and is close to tears;
Julian, prematurely decayed,
with hair and skin both gone grey;
and Loukas, who looks
quite the scholar on the face of it:
his gaze is faintly pompous,
and faint hieroglyphs
attend him obscurely at each side.
So many new faces for
the same old story!
Looking, we think of them as touching,
or as vain, or as beside
the point, depending
on our views; but then we return to
sunshine, blind and blinking, as
they, of course, cannot.
They lived in a time and place where death
was already an art form,
an old observance,
and died for what they could not foresee—
us, the future—things that have
come to light at last.

The Sound of the Sun

It makes one all right, though you hadn't thought of it,
A sound like the sound of the sky on fire, like Armageddon,
Whistling and crackling, the explosions of sunlight booming
As the huge mass of gas rages into the emptiness around it.
It isn't a sound you are often aware of, though the light speeds
To us in seconds, each dawn leaping easily across a chasm
Of space that swallows the sound of that sphere, but
If you listen closely some morning, when the sun swells
Over the horizon and the world is still and still asleep,
You might hear it, a faint noise so far inside your mind
That it must come from somewhere, from light rushing to darkness,
Energy burning towards entropy, towards a peaceful solution,
Burning brilliantly, spontaneously, in the middle of nowhere,
And you, too, must make a sound that is somewhat like it,
Though that, of course, you have no way of hearing at all.

An Arrangement of Sunlight at Hagia Sophia

"Not illuminated by the sun, but generated within,"
Says Procopius, referring to the radiance.
The dome seems to float above a ring of light,
And the sunbeams, all we know of heaven,
Cross and recross in their descent, amplifying
Each other and casting complex shadows,
Shifting in pattern with the time of day.
The system of support, admitting so much light,
Is burdened to its extreme, and the columns
Shed fine flakes of stone in their distress.

Hagia Sophia, an unorthodox construction,
Was imagined by Anthemius and Isidore, both Greeks,
At the behest of Justinian and with the grace of God.
In points of design, in the question of funding,
Sometimes an angel was required to intervene.
Even so, there have been accidents.
In May of 558, the dome itself collapsed;
But the fallen portions are always rebuilt,
Redesigned or replicated according to circumstances,
Producing slow motion across fourteen hundred years.

Ottoman Turks razed the atrium, raised four minarets,
And the golden tessellation, representing heaven,
Has largely been destroyed. It is miraculous
That the structure itself survives, withstanding
Over two hundred earthquakes and having suffered
Invading armies to ride right to its altar.
Yet the church stands as it has for centuries,
Approximating our own intentions and design,
Bearing the marks of our own mutability:
A realization, an idea insisted upon.

A Palaeologan Apology

In my city, grass grows over the old quarters,
The rain slides unobstructed through palace roofs;
Today, tomorrow, will bring barbarians to the gate.
These things are not things to think about.
The mind beholds them and stubbornly snaps shut.
We have made our monuments differently of late—
Our thoughts are more than versions of our lives,
And our reflections are more than mirrors.
We breathe the air of the only art there is:
If I should add a descant to a melody,
Rework a hymn that has been old five hundred years,
I share interpretations set down once by saints.
Multitudes have shed their lives for me.
The eloquent lines my ancestors drew
Rude hands imitate in every land I know:
Our own expressions will resurface someday in paint.
It is not hard to live in the world. We have no choice.
What we labor long to make is what will last . . .
If I break into song, generations give their voice.
We are ceremonious, and live in evidence of the past.

M31 in Andromeda

To the naked eye, it is all but invisible, a pale patch
Of nebulous starlight among a host of greater luminaries,
But on close consideration, it assumes magnified significance,
Comprising constellations and their worlds of difference.
With the human talent for noticing much, explaining little,
Stellar Body M31 was long remarked for an odd imbalance,
Revolving in mysterious concert with its own dark motives.
The hidden motivation turns out to be ourselves, our Milky Way,
And as matter may be defined by influence if not appearance,
The faint star became a galaxy, seen for what once it was.

What passes for present time there, across a gulf so vast
It can be bridged only by the lightning intangible of light,
We, here, have no way of knowing, but to us it appears
Extraordinarily beautiful, although it must be remembered
That beauty is in the eye and so in this case exists largely
In lenses, in the mirror images of scientific equipment.
The great gathering of light spins majestically in space,
Centrifugal force and the force of gravity conspiring
To yield configuration, an elegant ellipse, though why
To turn in emptiness, in absence of light or any warmth,
Should form anything is not easy to imagine, any more than why
Our own thoughts and dreams should take shape out of darkness.

The galaxy involves perhaps two hundred billion suns,
And it might reassure us, create some form of consolation,
That something so gigantic should seem so self-contained;
But the image comes at such remove that our quiet conclusions
Drop in the abyss of distance like stones in the wide sea.
Two million light-years out into space, back into time,
Far, far from us, the galaxy turns upon itself, and we,
As is our habit, have given it a name: Andromeda, a word
First given to that part of the sky by Greek astronomers,
Who thought the stars were bright reflections on themselves.

At a distance of what is, from our perspective, many years,
It is difficult now to separate whatever may once have happened
From all that certainly did not, but it seems Andromeda
Was a woman so beautiful she was set out on a rock, bound
Beside the sea and with a sea of stars over her head,
There to satisfy something terrible, something that no one,
Not her father, who was king, nor her father's priests,
Nor we who read the tale, had any real hope of averting
Or could think to comprehend.

Christ Pantocrator in San Giorgio dei Greci

I opened my eyes long ago in another city,
Regarding with a dispassionate expression
The business end of a paintbrush.
The first face I saw was wonderful,
As dreamy-eyed as I was unimpressed:
The artist had starved himself for days
Preparing the high dome of my forehead,
The impossible gesture of my right hand.
Since then faces have come and gone,
And the thick smoke of incense has settled
As softly as the veil of memory settles.
I know there are small saints beside me
In poor condition. I forget their names;
The words they spoke I have forgotten.
I know the gold leaf behind me is light,
I feel its bright suffusion of my features;
And the darkness I gaze out upon—
This dim church, the centuries, your face—
That, too, to me is as light, blazing
And impenetrable, divine on the face of it.

Filippo Brunelleschi, Florence, 1425

It was an execution in a lead-backed mirror,
A panel painted to illustrate a point
Of perspective: that parallel lines
In nature seem to converge and vanish,
That scenic views and constructed faces
Suffer exact diminution in our eyes.

You created an illusion for startled eyes,
Drawing the image from a small square mirror
Set up on the Duomo steps where it faces
The Baptistry. You marked the central point
Where perceptions could be made to vanish
And traced the building in geometric lines.

It seems to have been done along the lines
Of an exhibition—all those curious eyes
In the piazza! Later, your panel would vanish,
And there was, of course, no hope for the mirror.
But our accounts are precise, up to a point:
We know you held the proof up to their faces.

Imagine the expectation on their faces
As they queued up in impatient lines.
You drilled a peephole at the center point
Of the panel, and soon each pair of eyes
Saw your illusion reflected in the mirror,
Then reality appear, the mirror vanish.

Words are quickly said and quickly vanish:
If you addressed the crowd, their faces
Reflected back in miniature in your mirror,
We can only guess the content . . . some lines
From Dante, your favorite? Your eyes,
Too, perceived radiations from a central point.

Your exposition was brief and to the point.
In no time at all your audience would vanish
To try other mirrors with inquisitive eyes.
To this day, though, our prestressed faces
Are structures simply built along your lines.
Filippo, your past remains our mirror.

You taught us to hold mirrors to our eyes,
That single points possess so many faces;
The fine lines stretch to infinity and vanish.

In the Flemish Gallery

That one is wan and transparently out of this world
Does not make him less beautiful, less luminous,
And that the other is terribly still and says nothing
Does not make her reflection any less our own.
In Bruges, on a March day in 1505, each glowing instant,
Even this instant, is a chill breath away from death,
Is clothed in bright array and hides an inmost thought.
That is why the angel seems abstracted as he speaks;
That is why the woman is beside herself, imagining.
The clear bright blue that adorns the dead of winter
Still floats above mountains painted in the distance,
And the river remains frozen beneath delicate clouds.
On a March day in Bruges, spring might come at any hour,
But this angel will watch his words unravel into ages,
And the woman must pause an eternity over her reply.
It is a moment that might be lived forever, lingering
Like second thoughts or a melancholy angel, like us—
Look, the town beyond the bridge is one where we might live,
With its medieval walls and maze of interwoven streets;
See, there we are, among the crowd gathered in the square,
In Bruges, in the bitter winter of 1505.

E Pur Si Muove

Of course it had been madness even to bring it up,
Sheer madness, like the sighting of sea serpents
Or the discovery of strange lights in the sky;
And plainly it had been worse than madness to insist,
To devote entire treatises and a lifetime to the subject,
To a thing of great implication but no immediate use,
A thing that could not be conceived without study,
Without years of training and the aid of instruments,
And especially the delicate instrument of an open mind;
It had been stubbornness, foolishness, you see that now,
And so when the time comes you are ready to acquiesce,
When you have had your say, told the truth one last time,
You are ready to give the matter over and say no more.
When the time comes, you will take back your words,
But not because you fear the consequences of refusal
(Who looks into the night sky and imagines a new order
Has already seen the instruments of torture many times),
Though this is the conclusion your inquisitors will draw
And it is true you are not what is called a brave man;
And not because you are made indifferent in your contempt
(You take their point, agree with it even, that there is
Nothing so dangerous as a new way of seeing the world);
Rather, you accept the conditions lightly, the recantation,
Lightly you accept their offer of a villa with a view,
Because you have grown old and contention makes you weary,
Because you like the idea of raising vines and tomatoes,
And because, whatever you might have said or suffered,
It is in motion still, cutting a great arc through nothingness,
Sweeping through space according to a design so grand
It remains, just as they would have it, a matter of faith,
Because, whether you say yea, whether you say nay,
Nevertheless it moves.

Antimatter

Imagine a world where what we take for negative
Is seen as positive, where the charges that repel us
Become attractive, where our desperation is delight;
Imagine a photographic negative of life on earth,
Where images are all reversed, where bankers dress
In pin-striped red, and fast women all wear blue;
Think of a universe taking place in the interstices
Of ours, the very opposite of our grim fabulations,
An alternative occurring every instant and everywhere;
Think of things as Paul Dirac imagined them in 1935.
Perhaps such a world exists, although the evidence
Is slight, is found only in evanescences that hover
At the periphery of what we see, unstable particles
Equally intangible to the fantastic idea itself;
But suppose that place exists, and the possibilities
That have leaked out of this life are abundant there,
The future otherwise, the people different than what we are.
If you could find it, could reach that necessary place,
It would, of course, explode, destroying itself and you,
For the world of antimatter is fragile as the one we know;
But O suppose that world exists, within us, around us,
A world to balance the imperfections we have made,
An inaccessible, bizarre utopia with its own objects,
Subject to other laws, fated to another end, pursuing
Some other vision concomitant with our own.

About Planck Time

Once upon a time, way back in the infinitesimal
First fraction of a second attending our creation,
A tiny drop containing all of it, all energy
And all its guises, burst upon the scene,
Exploding out of nothing into everything
Virtually instantaneously, the way our thoughts
Leap eagerly to occupy the abhorrent void.
Once, say ten or twenty billion years ago,
In Planck time, in no time at all, the veil
Available to our perceptions was flung out
Over space at such a rate the mere imagination
Cannot keep up, so rapidly the speed of light
Lags miraculously behind, producing a series
Of incongruities that has led our curiosity,
Like Ariadne's thread, through the dim labyrinth
Of our conclusions to the place of our beginning.
In Planck time, everything that is was spread so thin
That all distance is enormous, between each star,
Between subatomic particles, so that we are composed
Almost entirely of emptiness, so that what separates
This world, bright ball floating in its midnight blue,
From the irrefutable logic of no world at all
Has no more substance than the traveller's dream,
So that nothing can be said for certain except
That sometime, call it Planck time, it will all just
Disappear, a parlor trick, a rabbit back in its hat,
Will all go up in a flash of light, abracadabra,
An idea that isn't being had anymore.

III

The Old Way of Telling Time

As all things pass and as everything in time becomes abstract, a quick
look around tells you that whatever limits you construct contract
so that soon you notice the walls closing in and the sandy
surface unsettling beneath you. In effect the motion
is like the little whirlpool formed by a basin
as it drains, and if you maintain enough
self-control you can sometimes hear
the gurgling sound, insidious
and obliviously inhuman.
The day comes when
there is not
even an
in
-
stant—
only a vacuum,
a falling sensation,
which can precede feelings
of freedom, as a corpse cut down
from a scaffold crumples to the earth,
or as wind roaring out of a canyon discovers
itself sweeping the plain. And so perhaps there is
some substance accumulating out of ourselves, even as we
are aware of losing our grip, and a final balance is arrived at
incorporating the passage of time and laws like gravity, an impassive
recompense, the pliable beauty given the wave-beaten and wind-driven sands.

Six of One

Of course, it may well be that the mind is of finite
Capacity as it is of finite space, so that
There comes a time when it will not hold any more
And whatever facts, figures, and nagging thoughts
We continue to cram into it, what with night school
And the learning of something new every day,
Must be balanced, must be given room enough,
And that this is what the meticulous mechanism
Of memory and its forgetfulness is for.
In this event, all the subconscious area left over,
The millions of brain cells swarming and hiving,
Buzzing like bees under summer sun, occupies itself
With things that can't quite be called thoughts,
Things like emotions, like interminable boredom,
Sitting vast in the mind but too vacuous to be
An idea, instead just a gesture, or a sort of sense,
And therefore is the piece of mind given to thought
A mere fraction of the whole, more like a baseball,
Probably, than a melon, i.e., we haven't really
Come all that far since the days of the dinosaur,
Terrible lizard. It would stand to reason, then,
That the precious little bundle of nerves is crucial,
That increments of intelligence make worlds of difference,
But in truth our own discrepancies don't matter much,
Since the professor may be absentminded, the idiot
May be a savant, and since many of us are dumb-lucky
Or too smart for our own good. Thus, although no one
Seriously believes it of himself, all of us are born
Equal to one another more than we know and equal
To little else, neither the love of women, held
In the tremulous hands like something fragile, nor
The love of language, words turned on the tongue;

And thus the poem arises out of a chance accumulation,
Out of a mind that perhaps achieved optimum content
Months or even years ago, say one morning in winter
When the sky was so blue and steam rose off the ocean
Into the other element of air.

Its Bladder-Like Sail

'' . . . she sent postcards
to only the nicer animals.''

a livid
and seemingly synthetic hue
of burgundy or murex or midnight blue,
it drifts in temperate seas
   as in irons, the ruffled float
   riffling in the breeze,

while below
trailing polyps hang like thin crepe
ribbons, descending fifty feet in the deep
to decorate an abyss
   with the only desire it knows,
   desire to digest.

In that web
the creatures caught dissolve piecemeal
as their passive host dissects them fin from scale,
those tentacles a womb where
   ontogeny capitulates,
   angel and trigger

fish, tetras,
carp, barbs, butterfly fish and blues,
all devolving to the primordial ooze
on which *Physalia* feeds.
   The bright bits strung in its tresses
   serve as lures to lead

fresh prospects
within arm's reach, there to be undone
by all that glitters; the lightest touch can stun
a man, let alone a fish,
   raising welts, causing fever, shock
   and paralysis

sufficient
to induce an "interference
with heart and lung action." Given such defense,
its natural enemies
    are few, and the Portuguese floats
    in vast colonies

half a mile
wide through warm latitudes and in
our Gulf Stream, islands of color which have been
described as "grotesque" and "lush."
    In the silent grottoes beneath
    those shores, one small fish

noses through
the gossamers, safe from their sting:
the man-of-war fish, almost immune, nibbling
the polyps of its predator,
    fed and housed and sometimes eaten
    by the man-of-war.

Electrocuting an Elephant

Her handlers, dressed in vests and flannel pants,
   Step forward in the weak winter light
Leading a behemoth among elephants,
Topsy, to another exhibition site;
   Caparisoned with leather bridle,
Six impassive tons of carnival delight
Shambles on among spectators who sidle
   Nervously off, for the brute has killed
At least three men, most recently an idle
Hanger-on at shows, who, given to distilled
   Diversions, fed her a live cigar.
Since become a beast of burden, Topsy thrilled
The crowds in her palmy days, and soon will star
   Once more, in an electrocution,
Which incident, though it someday seem bizarre,
Is now a new idea in execution.

Topsy has been fed an unaccustomed treat,
   A few carrots laced with cyanide,
And copper plates have been fastened to her feet,
Wired to cables running off on either side;
   She stamps two times in irritation,
Then waits, for elephants, having a thick hide,
Know how to be patient. The situation
   Seems dreamlike, till someone throws a switch,
And the huge body shakes for the duration
Of five or six unending seconds, in which
   Smoke rises and Topsy's trunk contracts
And twelve thousand mammoth pounds finally pitch
To earth, as the current breaks and all relax.
   It is a scene shot with shades of grey—
The smoke, the animal, the reported facts—
On a seasonably grey and gloomy day.

Would you care to see any of that again?
    See it as many times as you please,
For an electrician, Thomas Edison,
Has had a bright idea we call the movies,
    And called on for monitory spark,
Has preserved it all in framed transparencies
That are clear as day, for all the day is dark.
    You might be amused on second glance
To note the background—it's an amusement park!—
A site on Coney Island where elephants
    Are being used in the construction,
And where Topsy, through a keeper's negligence,
Got loose, causing some property destruction,
    And so is shown to posterity,
A study in images and conduction,
Sunday, January 4th, 1903.

El Niño

When the Boy appeared mysteriously
One spring, Pedro remarked that the seasons
Had lost track of themselves, had grown confused,

So that afternoons grew colder even
As he planted maize, and the sun could not
Be counted on as before. When the Boy

Came, the new leaves on the cacao trees
Withered almost at once, and the small rain
That fell to water the coffee berries

Descended with unusual violence,
Hurling the terraced hills into ravines
And washing entire plantations away.

Rosa-Maria bought a large candle
And attended an extra mass each day,
But once the Boy had come, the winter wind

Came, too, came unexpectedly in June,
Freezing birds and killing the crops with frost.
Rosa gave extra money to the priest,

But the high pastures remained mired in mud,
And the huge rain forest that lay beyond
The mountains was rumored to suffer drought.

Animals came out of the undergrowth
By day and sat by the side of the road
Blinking their gentle eyes in amazement,

And even the ocean currents altered,
So that strange fish no one had ever seen
Washed up each night and rotted on the beach.

When the Boy came, the stars forgot themselves;
Cows all dropped their calves in January
After the Boy appeared, and Rosa prayed

To the Virgin to bring the red moon back
To its senses and stop the army ants.
But Pedro said the Boy had other plans,

Said his ideas were other than our own,
His way of seeing the sunlight, his way
Of understanding a tree. Pedro said

That El Niño had simply changed his mind,
Had tired of this world and begun to dream
Another dream of how this world should be.

Committed to Memory

The landscape was surprisingly sparse. Each day
New people arrived, buildings were erected, foliage

Was planted in swaths; but nothing could stay put.
Plants withered, elaborate buildings wandered away,

And the people lay down and died. It must have been
The climate, though it seemed temperate enough . . .

The sun was always setting with a modest display,
And the rain of happiness, of misery, never fell.

But the air was what you had once breathed,
Once found necessary, sitting on the verandah

Regarding the pleasant view and treacherous terrain.
You were with a woman wearing a silk evening gown,

And you watched the auburn hair shadowing her face,
Her delicate mouth speak words she knew you would forget.

Light Falls on the Man

"Light falls on the man, but he does not become it."—Alfred Corn

Not without some equivocation, anyway, not
Without great pain: put a man into an oven
And the flesh will bubble, blacken, burst to flame
And shed some light, though what it illuminates
Is not what we would see. Irradiate a man
And instruments delicate enough may perceive light,
Borrowed perhaps, but lingering, blossoming
Like foxfire along the dark pathways of the body.
Light falls on the man, but he becomes nothing,
His small energies insignificant to that around him,
Gold light of the sun, cold light of the moon.
The light falls, and we struggle to be like it,
Though what light we shed warms nothing, makes
Nothing grow, brings up nothing out of the earth.
Light fallen upon us, we walk out into the sun,
Raising our arms in rays that will not harm us much,
Trying for a transparency at any rate, like glass,
Like the human eye, that the light shine through us,
That we hold nothing back.

The Life of Stars

I. STELLAR OCCASIONS

Nothing, of course, is absolute, nothing,
Neither time, nor distance, neither darkness,
Silence, absence, stillness, nor emptiness,
Nor temperature in blank space—nothing—
And so it is we must at last have these,
Must, when each equation has made its run
For infinity and found its fraction,
Have these, to consume themselves by degrees
And thrive for lack of all alternative,
To compose themselves out of dust and live
And shed life, to shine or not in their way,
To demonstrate a form of self-control,
Dividing light from dark, the night from day:
Red giant, blue giant, white dwarf, black hole.

II. RED GIANT

Comes a time when the spirit expands, waxing eloquently,
Pushing back previous limits and stretching into darkness.
The time comes at last when the self begins lumining large,
Candescent with the glow of so much accumulated living,
With layers of memory and the heated atmosphere of emotion.
There comes a time, and we assume shades of dazzling color,
The burnish of gold and of bronze, the blush of ripe fruit,
The brilliance of a sun as it quenches itself in the sea.
In time, others observe the illuminations, our emanation,
Searching the heavens for the source of such extravagance,
And we think, how beautiful, consummately beautiful, although
We know it is only the light of a heart exhausting itself,
Guttering, the flare of the soul as it burns itself out.
A pale flame leaps high on the shadow wall of space.
Everybody is a star.

III. BLUE GIANT

It is the grand conception, to burn brightly,
To coalesce out of nebulous beginnings and ignite,
To turn every element at hand to the one idea, to burn
Hugely, magnificently, a short time and at great heat,
To stand as a beacon in space and thrust the blue flame
Of the one idea into the very depths of the abyss,
To make a conflagration out of the self, to shed
The shimmering light of the self over every distance,
To flash spontaneously into fusion and burn intensely
For the brief moment (6 million? 60 million years?),
To ignite out of a magnitude of self and burn intensely
At incalculable heat (60 million? 600 million degrees?),
To stand on the brink of extinction and bluely burn,
To fuel the flames of the great conceit, to burn bright
With the obsession of the self, to be the blue giant,
To mesmerize every eye, to burn and burning grasp
The unimaginable, catastrophic end.

IV. WHITE DWARF

One day it occurred to you, who had known no day
Beyond the glowing moment of your bright effusion,
That your every occasion had been one for bitterness,
Your ends all conclusions foregone these many years;
Who had known long life, unearthly beauty, you came
To think of this one day and became a timid thing.
You had asked for the heavens, and they were yours,
Yours to shine in, to inflame with your desires,
But the void was insatiable, desired more than you.
You had wanted the world, and it was given you,
Many worlds in fact, yours to nourish or destroy,
But worlds proved no use, and you deserted each.
If there were other possibilities, they were not yours,
Who had bent every effort to arrive at this alone,
At the day that dawned suddenly when you discovered
Yourself as an Everyman in some grim morality play,
Yourself as a shining example of ultimate decay,
A parody of youth and its projects, the day you came
Down to this, a shrivelled thing, the white dwarf.

V. BLACK HOLE

At the edge of space, at the edge of the mind, where
All instruments become objects of surmise, and where
All idea becomes pure theory, there may be, although
The evidence is circumstantial, circumspect at best,
There might just be a minute abyss, or many of them,
Stars collapsing on themselves, fantastically shrunken,
Tiny spheres of immense attraction called black holes.
Physicists, who are not normally given to playing fast
With the facts, believe, or some of them, that these
Are ravenous for the rest of creation, gulping particles
Of light and matter, compressing entire solar systems
Into something no larger than a golf ball, and yielding
No notice of themselves beyond their apparent absence.
So great their gravity, according to such speculation,
So dense the kernel at their core, that black holes
Permit nothing to escape their grasp, no expression
Of energy whatever, and so remain invisible, sites
Of ultimate darkness, the unseen hands in the universe.
All this, of course, could clear up a lot of questions,
Such as why empty areas of space exert such influence,
And how it is such empty areas exist to begin with,
Not to mention what's on the other side of the rainbow
And where light goes when it dies; in fact, black holes
Might explain almost anything, and some physicists
Have even suggested that if so much is made to vanish
From our universe, it must all reemerge somewhere else,
Must all fountain forth into another place and time,
And even that man, endlessly resourceful, might someday
Reach other states by travelling through black holes.
Physicists, some of them, who are not normally given
To playing loose with the figures, have said all this,

Which proves that physicists may be intoxicated, too,
With the imagined thing, with stars and the firmament,
But proves also that when human answers are exhausted,
The nymph beside the spring, the spirit of the place,
When all the comforting myths have been seen through,
The mind finds other solutions, dark and irresistible,
And sets them in the sky to reign from there.

A Cock to Asklepios

When the ceremonial ship has returned to port,
Bearing certain satisfactions for others
And its portion of suffering for you;
When you have spoken a last time with those
Who condemn you and remained reasonably adamant;
When you have bid farewell to your household
And conversed thoughtfully with your friends;
When the sun of your last day is soon to set
And you have drunk the bitter cup to the lees—
What, finally, will remain for you to say?
You, who have succeeded in living honorably,
Who have devoted your entire life to an exactitude
Of thought and word, who have known most of what
It is permitted to know, what words can you find now?
Kardia, when you settle on the bed you have chosen,
When you feel the chill advance from your extremities
And you cover even your face to die with dignity,
Then, as an aside, as an afterthought almost,
Make your peace with what cannot be known,
Balance your accounts with the darkness
To which you have given yourself.

Three People Reading Stevens in a Room

She bends over me, the woman with blue eyes
And gold-shot dress, her jewelled hand,
Bangles, turquoise rings, cool on my forehead—

So I have come to this room at last . . . *Be still*,
It is only coming out of sleep, the dreams
Indistinct, sky without stars during sunlight.

Several people painting windows on the walls,
The soft, balding man with a parrot on his shoulder,
The chill, descending breath of this woman:

Here in this unknown room at last . . . *Lie still*,
We will not welcome you, it is waking,
All along you were here, the dreams rising

From your eyes like steam, the words crouching
Under your tongue, your lips blue in the cold.
This room with the gold lettering on the door

And the mail slot taped shut . . . *Rest now*,
We will think your thoughts even when you go,
Thoughts of yourself, all you know of yourself.

Terms to Be Met

Of course, one way would be to resign yourself and join up,
The idea being that nobody would give it a second thought,
And that after a while it's any port in this kind of storm.
One way would be to join the Marines, to start taking orders,
To cloister yourself in a monastery and take vows of silence,
Working in God's garden while He tanned your shaved head.
You wouldn't really have to believe it, to believe anything,
That being part of the point, to have it put on a platter,
Fit conduct assigned, fit topics for thought already invented,
Your doubts all anticipated, refuted with consummate casuistry.
You could probably take pretty much the same pleasures, too,
Since the mind willfully construes conclusions out of thin air,
Since so much of inconsequence would simply be taken care of,
And thus no rationale obtains against our calm capitulation,
On some August day perhaps, in a clearing with clouds overhead.
But the rage for one's own thoughts cannot be suppressed,
The animal urge like the instinct for so much territory,
And each of us clutches his own idea through all extremity,
Though the landscape we find ourselves in isn't much support,
The sky having somehow backed off a bit, gone farther away,
Leaving us here, at the margins of the mind, where we must live.